NON - VERBAL REASONING 1
MULTIPLE CHOICE
PAPER 1

ALPHA SERIES
PRACTICE PAPERS

INSTRUCTIONS FOR PUPIL

1. In this paper there are three tests. The time allocated for each test varies but the instructions will tell you how long you have to complete the test. Do not open this booklet until told to do so.

2. Do not write your answers in this booklet. Draw a line in the box thus ▭ next to the correct answer in the answer booklet.

3. Use a pencil and if you make a mistake rub out your mark and then mark the correct box.

4. Work through the questions as quickly and as carefully as you can. Each question is worth one mark so do not spend too long on an individual question.

5. If you finish early, check your work and have another attempt at any questions you have not answered.

6. You are not allowed to ask questions during the test. If you do not understand something try your best with it then move on to the next question.

Similarities. The three shapes on the left of the page on each row all have something in common with each other even though they are all different shapes. Work out the similarities and then work out which of the five shapes under the letters A to E is similar to the three shapes. For your answer select the correct letter in your Answer Booklet.

Time allowed: 3 minutes 20 seconds

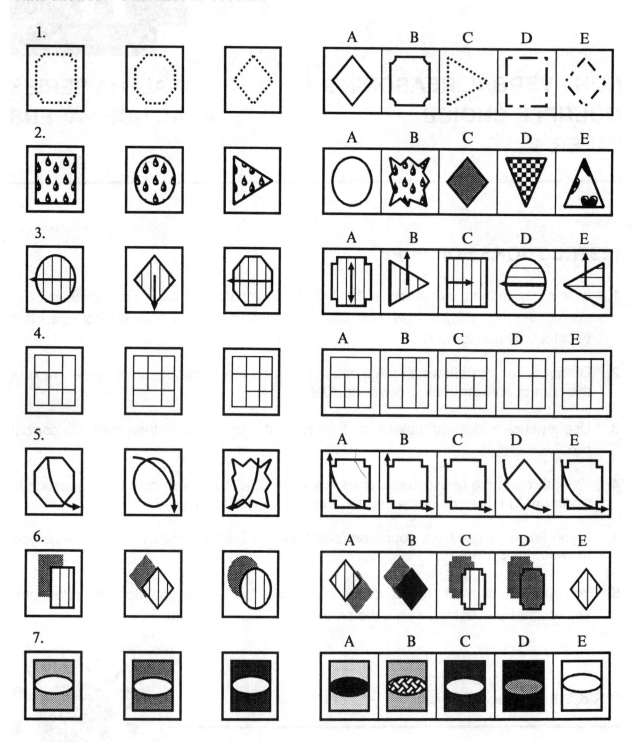

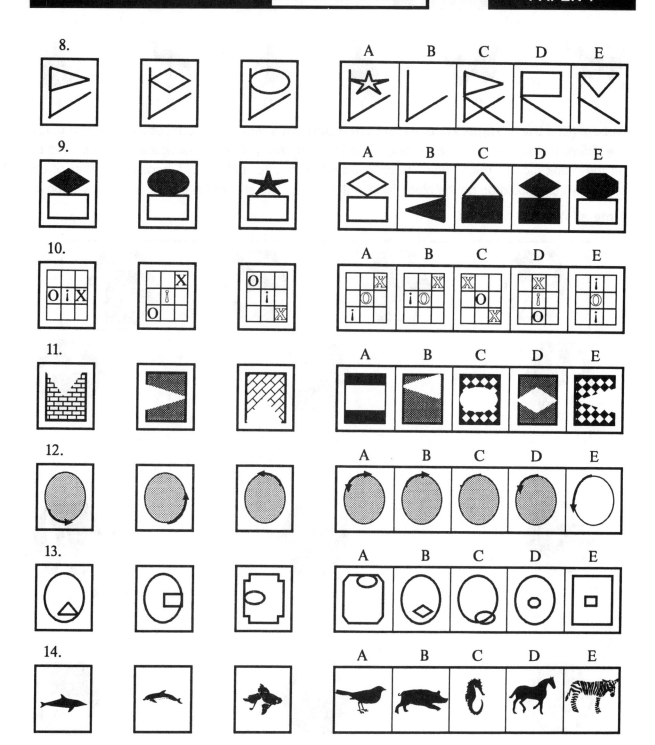

8.

9.

10.

11.

12.

13.

14.

END OF THE TEST
Do not turn over until you are told to do so.
Use any remaining time to check your answers

A   B   C   D   E   F

Cubes. (See the example sheet before attempting this test.) The four cubes in the box below are different views from the same dice. Use them to help you work out which animal should be on the blank side of each cube. Each animal has a letter below it. Choose the letter of the animal which should be on the blank face of the cube. The six animal shapes are shown above.

Time allowed: 8 minutes

1.

2.

3.

4.

5.

6.

7.

8.

9.

10.

11.

12.

13.

14.

15.

16.

17.

18.

19.

20.

21.

22.

23.

24.

END OF THE TEST
Do not turn over until you are told to do so.
Use any remaining time to check your answers

Shapes. The shape below and the one on the next page have had a grid placed on top of them. Each of the smaller shapes in the boxes will fit exactly into one grid of the larger shape. Work out the grid letter for each shape and select the letter of the grid position from the choice in the Answer Booklet. Some of the shapes are used more than once.

Time allowed: 2 minutes 10 seconds

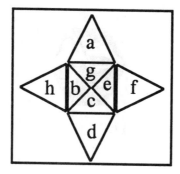

1.	2.	3.	4.
5.	6.	7.	8.
9.	10.	11 .	12.
13 .	14.	15.	16.

17.

18.

19.

20.

21.

22.

23.

24.

25.

26.

27.

28.

29.

30.

31 .

32.

END OF THE TEST
Do not turn over until you are told to do so.
Use any remaining time to check your answers

MARK SHEET PAPER 1

TEST	MAXIMUM	ACTUAL
Similarities	14	
Cubes	24	
Shapes	32	
TOTAL	**70**	

Published by:
R & S Educational Services • 23 Manor Square • Otley • West Yorkshire • LS21 3AP
Printed by - Chippendale Press • 65 Bondgate • Otley • West Yorkshire • LS21 3AB

NON - VERBAL REASONING 1
MULTIPLE CHOICE
PAPER 2

ALPHA SERIES
PRACTICE PAPERS

INSTRUCTIONS FOR PUPIL

1. In this paper there are three tests. The time allocated for each test varies but the instructions will tell you how long you have to complete the test. Do not open this booklet until told to do so.

2. Do not write your answers in this booklet. Draw a line in the box thus ⊟ next to the correct answer in the answer booklet.

3. Use a pencil and if you make a mistake rub out your mark and then mark the correct box.

4. Work through the questions as quickly and as carefully as you can. Each question is worth one mark so do not spend too long on an individual question.

5. If you finish early, check your work and have another attempt at any questions you have not answered.

6. You are not allowed to ask questions during the test. If you do not understand something try your best with it then move on to the next question.

Analogies. (See the example sheet before attempting this test.) Study the first two shapes in each row. The relationship between the third shape and one of the shapes in the boxes underneath the letters A to E is the same as the relationship between the first two shapes. Work out which of the five shapes has the same relation to the third shape as the second shape has to the first one and enter the correct letter into your Answer Booklet.

Time allowed: 5 minutes

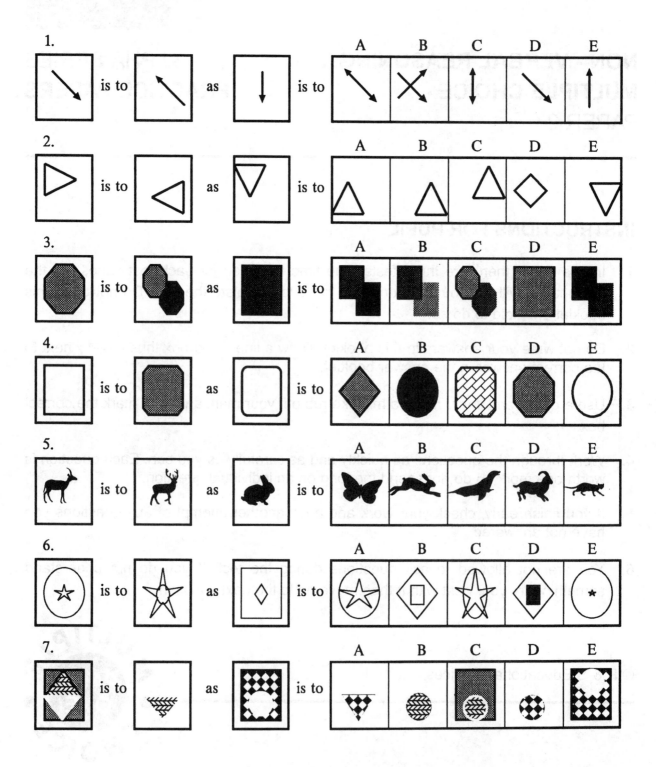

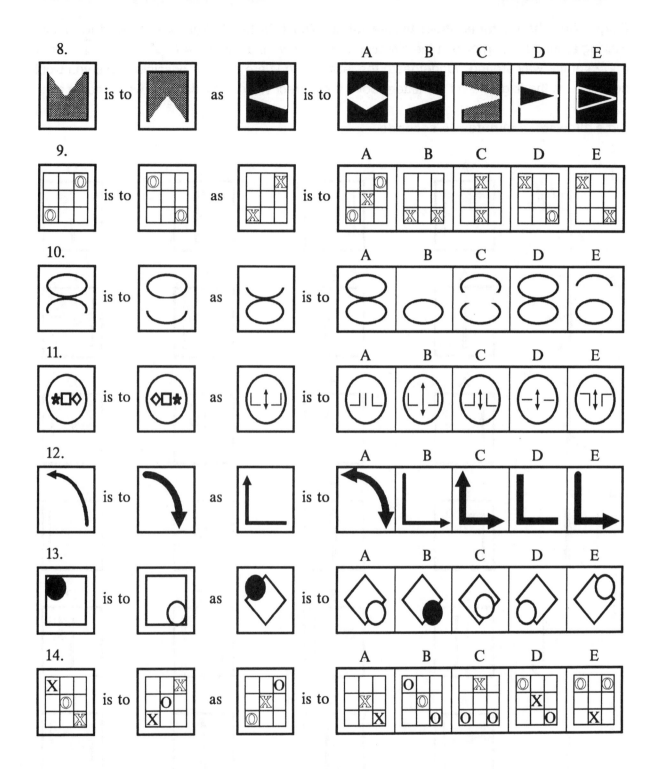

Flags. (See the example sheet before attempting this test.) You are required to imagine walking around the flag pole in the direction of the arrow and either ¹/4 (↗), ¹/2 (↻) or ³/4 (↻) of the way around. Underneath the letters A to D are the four possible views you would now have of the flag. Select the letter above the correct view of the flag you would now have.

Time allowed:　4 minutes 15 seconds

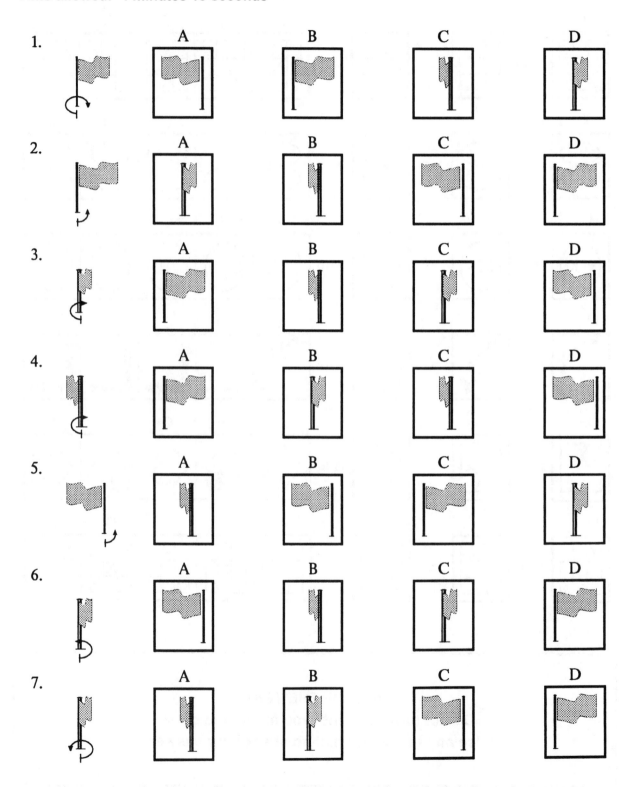

8.
   A   B   C   D

9.
   A   B   C   D

10.
   A   B   C   D

11.
   A   B   C   D

12.
   A   B   C   D

13.
   A   B   C   D

14.
   A   B   C   D

END OF THE TEST
Do not turn over until you are told to do so.
Use any remaining time to check your answers

Similarities. The three shapes on the left of the page on each row all have something in common even though they are all different shapes. Work out what they have in common and then work out which of the five shapes under the letters A to E is similar to the three shapes and select the correct letter in your Answer Booklet.

Time allowed: 2 minutes 30 seconds

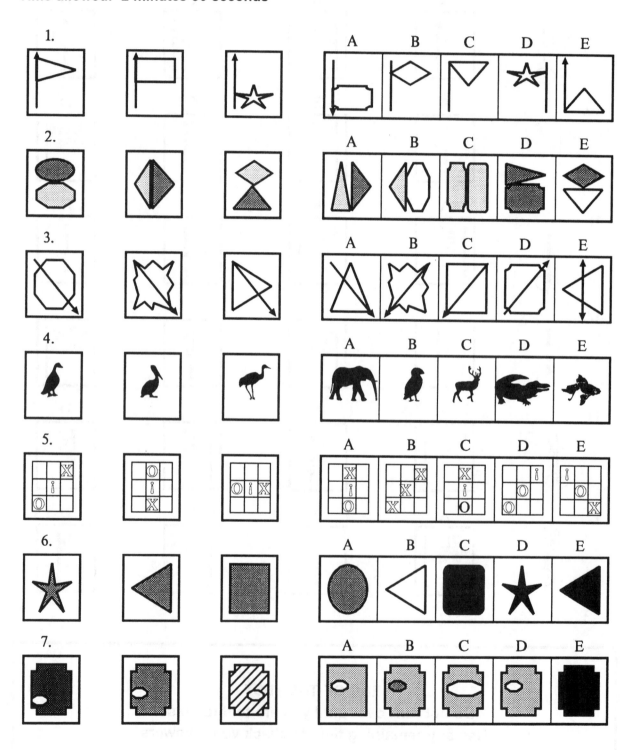

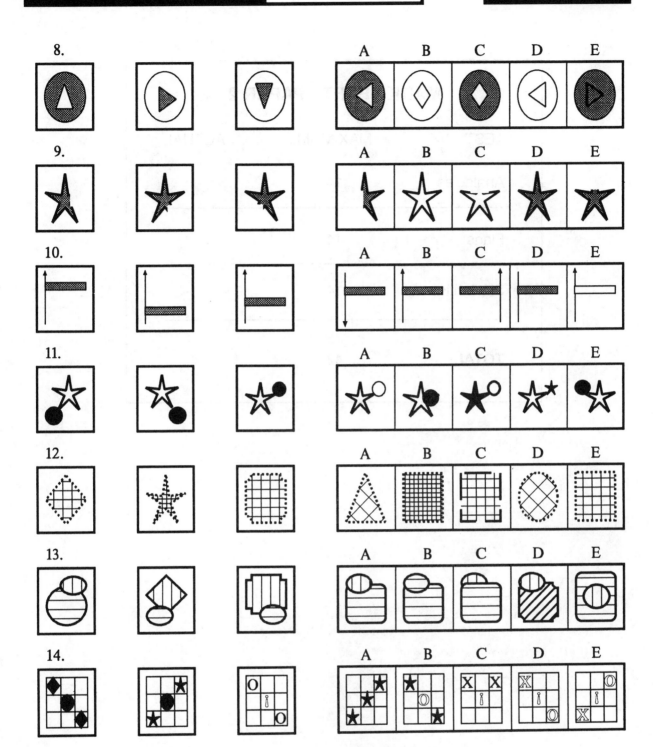

END OF THE TEST
Do not turn over until you are told to do so.
Use any remaining time to check your answers

MARK SHEET   PAPER 2

TEST	MAXIMUM	ACTUAL
Analogies	14	
Flags	14	
Similarities	14	
TOTAL	**42**	

Published by:
R & S Educational Services • 23 Manor Square • Otley • West Yorkshire • LS21 3AP
Printed by - Chippendale Press • 65 Bondgate • Otley • West Yorkshire • LS21 3AB

NON - VERBAL REASONING 1
MULTIPLE CHOICE
PAPER 3

ALPHA SERIES
PRACTICE PAPERS

INSTRUCTIONS FOR PUPIL

1. In this paper there are three tests. The time allocated for each test varies but the instructions will tell you how long you have to complete the test. Do not open this booklet until told to do so.

2. Do not write your answers in this booklet. Draw a line in the box thus ▭ next to the correct answer in the answer booklet.

3. Use a pencil and if you make a mistake rub out your mark and then mark the correct box.

4. Work through the questions as quickly and as carefully as you can. Each question is worth one mark so do not spend too long on an individual question.

5. If you finish early, check your work and have another attempt at any questions you have not answered.

6. You are not allowed to ask questions during the test. If you do not understand something try your best with it then move on to the next question.

Odd-One-Out. In each of the following questions, the five shapes are all different but four of them are similar to each other. Work out which shape is completely different to the other four shapes and mark your choice in the Answer Booklet.

Time allowed: 2 minutes 30 seconds

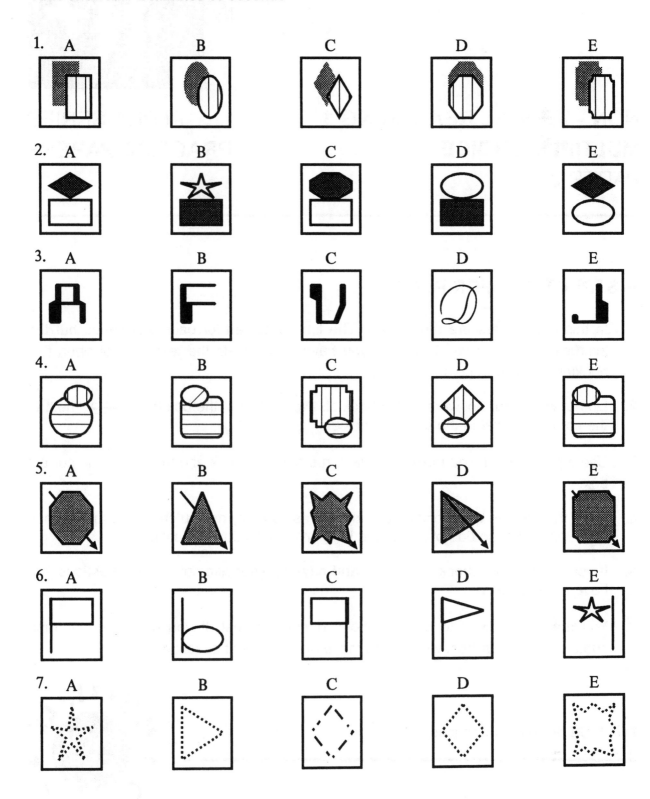

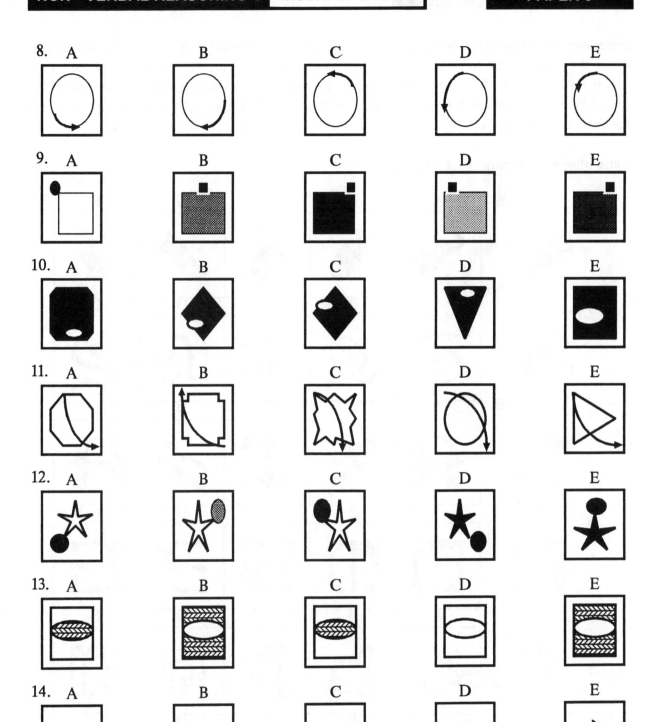

Rotation: (See the example sheet before attempting this test.) Only two of the five shapes inside the box on each row can be rotated or moved round to face the same way as the shape on the left of the box. The other three shapes are mirror images of the shape. Work out which two of the five shapes are the same as the shape on the left and select the two correct letters in the Answer Booklet.

Time allowed: 4 minutes 30 seconds

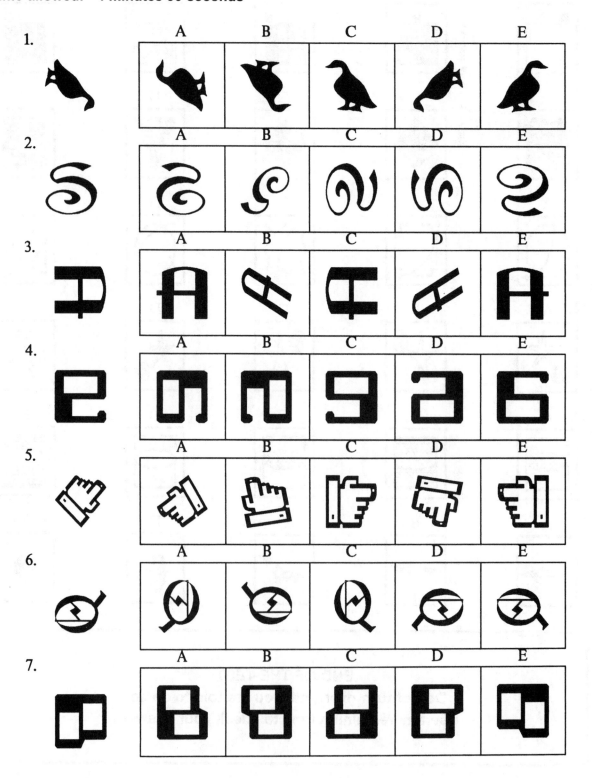

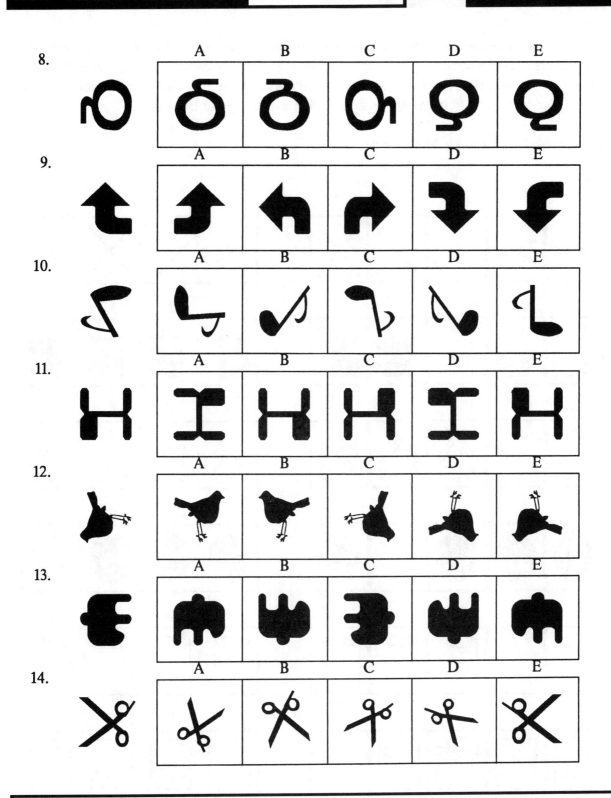

8. | A | B | C | D | E
9. | A | B | C | D | E
10. | A | B | C | D | E
11. | A | B | C | D | E
12. | A | B | C | D | E
13. | A | B | C | D | E
14. | A | B | C | D | E

END OF THE TEST
Do not turn over until you are told to do so.
Use any remaining time to check your answers

Series.   (See the example sheet before attempting this test.) The four shapes on the left of each row are part of a series but one shape is missing. Work out what is happening in the series and find the missing shape from the shapes below the letters A to D. Select the letter above the shape which is missing from the series and mark it in the Answer Booklet.

Time allowed: 4 minutes 30 seconds

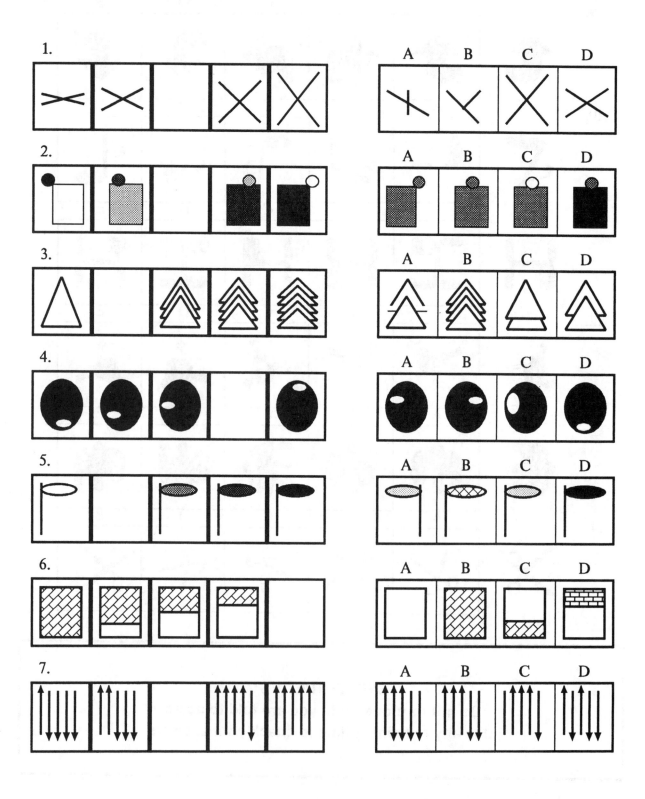

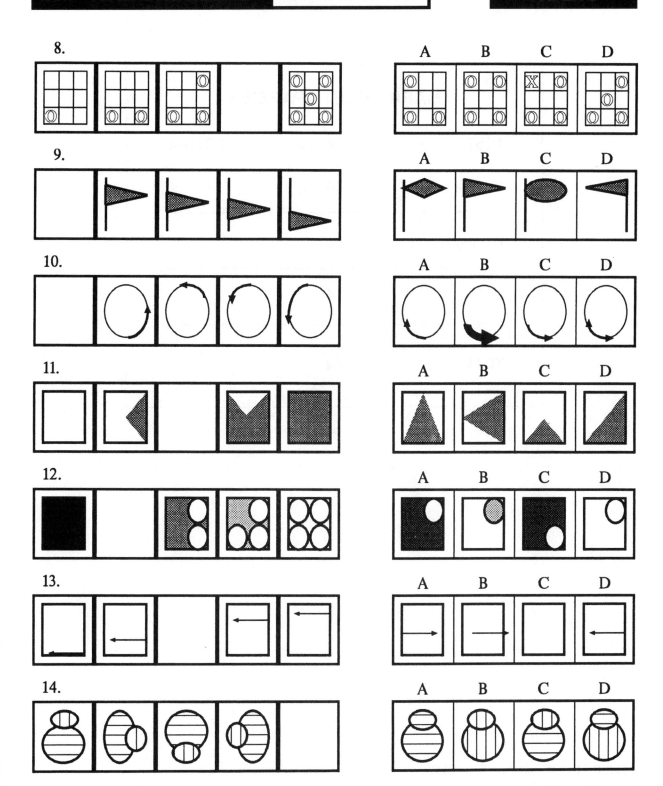

8. A B C D

9. A B C D

10. A B C D

11. A B C D

12. A B C D

13. A B C D

14. A B C D

END OF THE TEST
Do not turn over until you are told to do so.
Use any remaining time to check your answers

MARK SHEET   PAPER 3

TEST	MAXIMUM	ACTUAL
Odd-One-Out	14	
Rotation	14	
Series	14	
TOTAL	**42**	

© R & S EDUCATIONAL SERVICES
Alpha Series 1993
Non - Verbal Reasoning Pack 1   2001

Published by:
R & S Educational Services • 23 Manor Square • Otley • West Yorkshire • LS21 3AP
Printed by - Chippendale Press • 65 Bondgate • Otley • West Yorkshire • LS21 3AB

NON - VERBAL REASONING 1
MULTIPLE CHOICE
PAPER 4

ALPHA SERIES
PRACTICE PAPERS

INSTRUCTIONS FOR PUPIL

1. In this paper there are three tests. The time allocated for each test varies but the instructions will tell you how long you have to complete the test. Do not open this booklet until told to do so.

2. Do not write your answers in this booklet. Draw a line in the box thus ▭ next to the correct answer in the answer booklet.

3. Use a pencil and if you make a mistake rub out your mark and then mark the correct box.

4. Work through the questions as quickly and as carefully as you can. Each question is worth one mark so do not spend too long on an individual question.

5. If you finish early, check your work and have another attempt at any questions you have not answered.

6. You are not allowed to ask questions during the test. If you do not understand something try your best with it then move on to the next question.

Silhouettes. Study the shape on the left side of the page. Only one of the four shapes on its right is exactly the same shape but with the opposite colour. This means that the black parts of the shape become white and white parts become black. Choose the letter above the shape which is exactly the same as the one on the left but opposite in colour.

Time allowed: 2 minutes 45 seconds

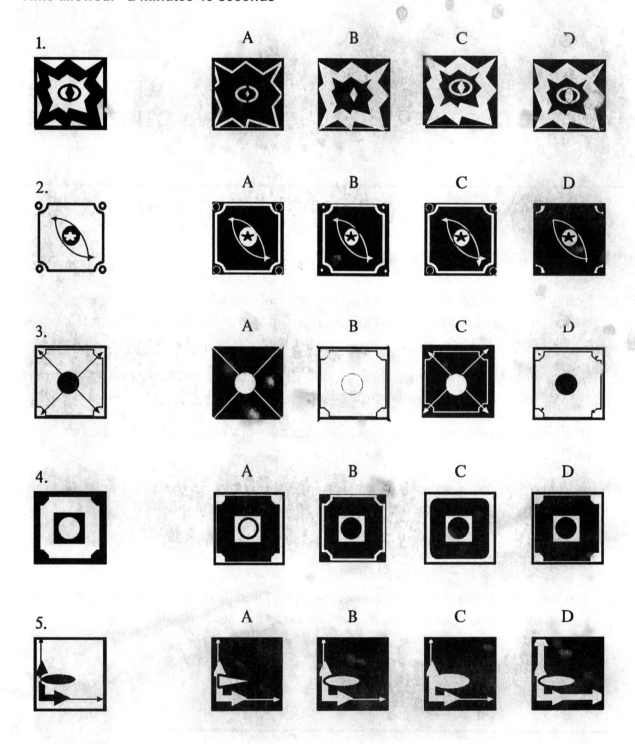

6.

A  B 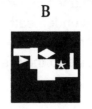 C 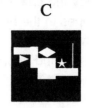 D

7.

A B C D

8.

A B C  D

9.

A B  C  D

10.

A B  C D

END OF THE TEST
Do not turn over until you are told to do so.
Use any remaining time to check your answers

Analogies. Study the first two shapes in each row. The relationship between the third shape and one of the shapes in the boxes underneath the letters A to E is the same as the relationship between the first two shapes. Work out which of the five shapes has the same relation to the third shape as the second shape has to the first one and choose the letter above it, mark your answer in the Answer Booklet.

Time allowed: 5 minutes

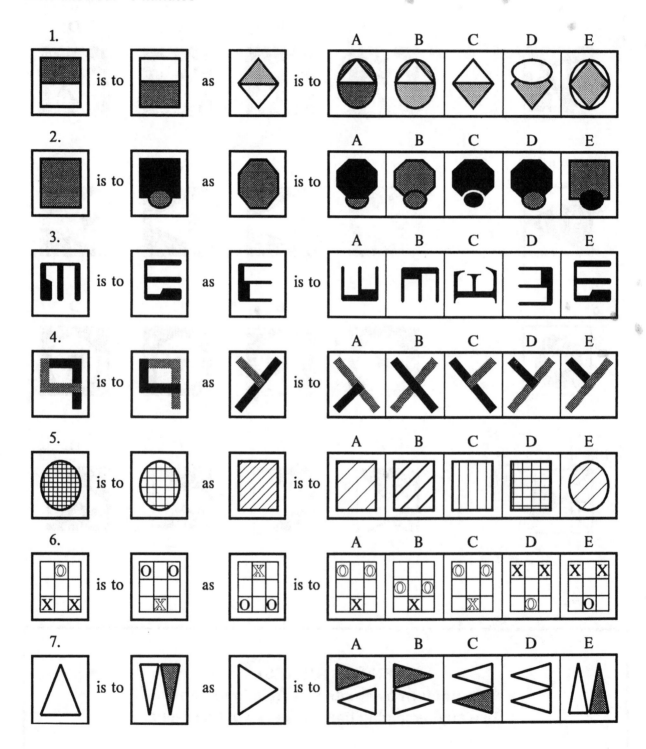

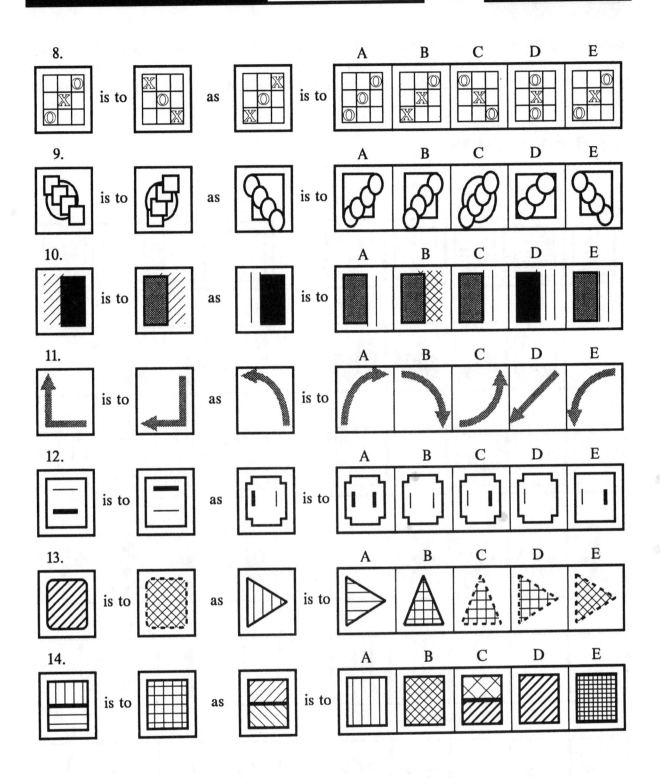

Series. The four shapes on the left of each row are part of a series but one shape is missing. Work out what is happening in the series and find the missing shape from the shapes below the letters A to D. Select the letter above the shape which is missing from the series and mark it in the Answer Booklet.

Time allowed: 4 minutes 30 seconds

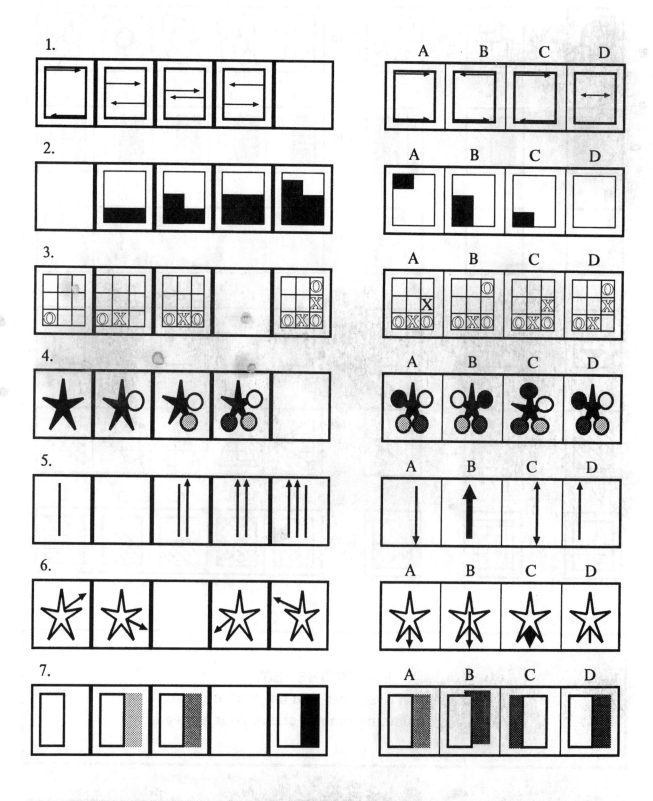

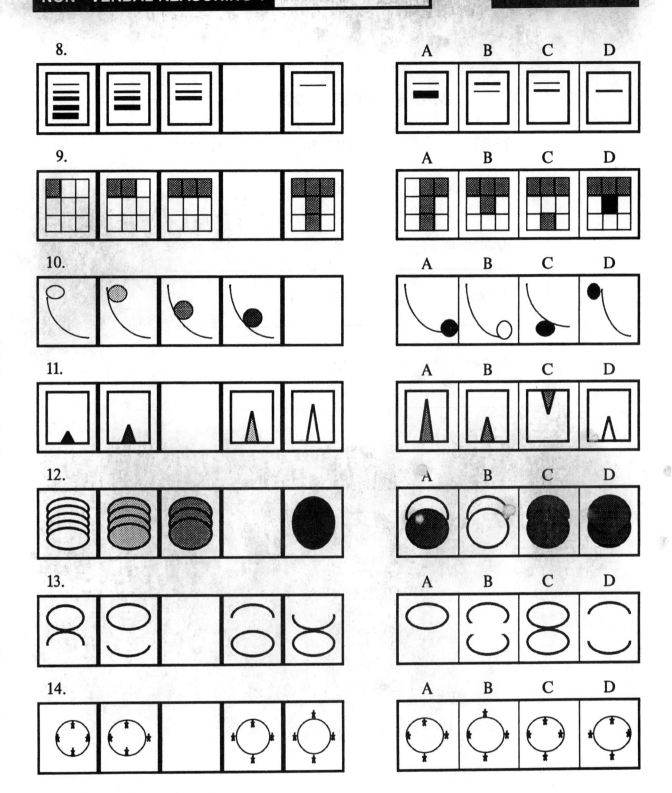

8.

9.

10.

11.

12.

13.

14.

END OF THE TEST
Do not turn over until you are told to do so.
Use any remaining time to check your answers

MARK SHEET   PAPER 4

TEST	MAXIMUM	ACTUAL
Silhouettes	10	
Analogies	14	
Series	14	
TOTAL	**38**	

Published by:
R & S Educational Services • 23 Manor Square • Otley • West Yorkshire • LS21 3AP
Printed by - Chippendale Press • 65 Bondgate • Otley • West Yorkshire • LS21 3AB

EXAMPLE SHEET

General Information

Each Paper consists of three tests. The time allowed for each test varies so that an adult with a stopwatch will need to time the candidate. We would suggest that each Paper be attempted in the same session: complete one test, allow perhaps five minutes break and then attempt the next test. We strongly suggest that only one Paper be attempted in any session with an interval of several days between each Paper.

We recommend you to read through the directions together and, if necessary, even use the first question of a test to demonstrate to your child what is required before s/he attempts the rest of the test unaided. In the examinations, the examiner will explain the task fully and sample questions will be attempted by the candidates, so this initial assistance is in no sense 'cheating'.

Most of the different types of tests will be sufficiently explained by the instructions but below we explain more fully with the help of examples those test types which children find particularly difficult. Some of the tests refer you to this example sheet and we advise you to look at each example with your child when that particular test type is being attempted.

Series

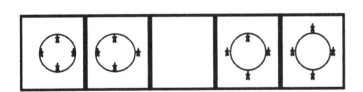 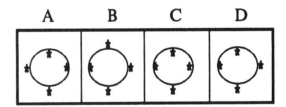

In the above example, we need to work out what is happening to the shapes on the left-hand side of the page. In the first box, four stars are enclosed within the circle. In the second box, we see that the right-hand star is now outside the circle. The third shape is missing so we have to look at the fourth and fifth box and try to work out what has happened. In the fourth box there are three stars outside the circle and in the fifth box all four stars are outside. Note that we have detected that one extra star is moved outside the circle in each box in a clockwise direction.

Looking at the four shapes on the right-hand side of the page, we can see that the shape under the letter 'C' only has one star outside. The shape underneath 'B' has three stars outside the circle so we can eliminate these two shapes. There are two stars outside the circle in the shape under 'A' but the first star has returned to inside the circle. Therefore 'D' must be the answer since the two stars are in the correct positions outside the circle. It only remains to choose the letter above the box and mark the answer in the Answer Booklet.

Analogies

Let us start with a verbal example: Little is to Large as Fat is to ?. We need to understand the analogy or relationship between the first two terms, Little and Large. The second term, Large, is the opposite of the first term, Little. We therefore need to find the opposite of the third term, Fat, which is obviously Thin. Now let us look at a non-verbal example.

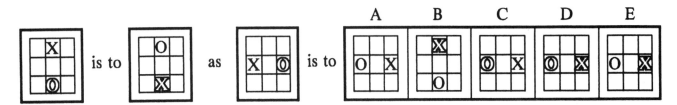

We can see in the first box that a black cross is placed vertically above the outlined nought in the grid. In the second box a black nought is above an outlined cross. The relationship appears to be that the nought and cross have been swapped but the shape which is on the bottom row of grids remains outlined. In the third box, the black cross and the outlined nought are facing each other horizontally. From the analogy of the first two shapes, we would expect the cross and the nought to be swapped and the outlined shape to remain on the right hand side of the grid.

If we look at the five shapes under the letters, we see that the shape under 'A' has the nought and cross where we would expect to see them but neither is outlined so this must be wrong. Under 'B', the cross is outlined, which we are looking for, but the two shapes are facing each other vertically, whereas we are looking for them to face each other horizontally, so 'B' is also wrong. Under 'C', the two characters are where we want them but the outline has also swapped places and means 'C' is wrong. Under 'D', the characters are both outlined so that this shape is wrong. Only under 'E' do we find what we are looking for. The nought and cross have been reversed but the outlined shape is still on the right-hand side of the grid, so the 'E' box should be marked in the answer booklet.

Cubes and Dice

The important thing with cubes is to try to 'picture' the cube rotating. Each question can be solved by reference to at least one of the four example cubes shown above the questions.

In this example, in order to help us find the missing shape, we first need to find either the stork on the top face or the butterfly on the front face from the example cubes. The only example cube which will help us is the fourth one where the stork is on the top face. To move the example cube to the same position as the cube with the blank face, we would need to turn it anti-clockwise by 90°. By 'picturing' the shapes on the cube, we see that the dog would move from the front face to the right-hand face, and therefore the answer would be the letter allocated to the dog.

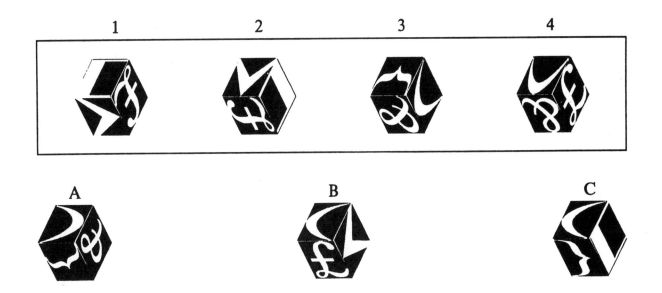

The four examples in the box are different views of the same cube. This type of exercise requires you to find the one view in each row which is from the same cube as in the example view 4. The principle is the same as for the animal cubes. This time it is helpful to eliminate the two wrong shapes rather than find the correct shape.

If we look at the first cube, 'A', we can see that the ')' symbol on the top face is also shown on example 4 but needs to be rotated by 90° clockwise. By doing this, we find that the '&' symbol moves from the right-hand face to the front face - as in the example cube 4. Unfortunately it remains the right way up whereas on the example view 4 it is upside down. We therefore know that this cube is false.

Cube 'B' can also be checked against the same example cube 4. This time, we have to move the '(' symbol 90° anti-clockwise. This has the effect of moving the '£' symbol from the front face to the right-hand face - as it is on the example cube 4. Furthermore, it is the right way up, which suggests it is the right cube. We could also check this cube against the second example cube 2 by rotating the '£' symbol by 90° anti-clockwise. This has the effect of moving the '<' symbol from the right-hand face to the top face, still facing the same way, which is the same as the example cube 2. Cube 'B' therefore could be the correct answer.

Moving on to the 'C' cube, we can again use example 4 to test it. In this case the '(' symbol on the top face needs to be rotated 90° anti-clockwise to face the same way as the same symbol on the same face of the example cube 4. This has the effect of moving the '}' symbol from the front face to the right-hand face. However, on the example cube, we find that face occupied by the '£' symbol. This cube is therefore wrong and so the correct cube is definitely 'B'.

Note that it is not necessary to prove the correct answer if you are certain that the other two views must be wrong.

1	2	3	4

Dice questions are solved in the same way as the cubes of symbols and animals in that they still need to be 'pictured' as they are rotated. The fact they are numerical however provides assistance in working out the blank faces. The sum of opposite faces always add up to 7. In other words, if one face is 5, we know that the opposite face is 7 - 5, that is 2. Let us use this information on the example of the die on the left of this writing. Looking at our four example dice, we see that the fourth one can be rotated so that the 1 moves from the top face to the front face. The 2 will stay on the same face but will be rotated so that it runs from top right to bottom left. The problem is to find what number will be on the top face. We know that it won't be the 4 because that has been moved from the front face to the bottom face which is hidden. However, we also know that if the 4 is on the bottom face then subtracting 4 from 7 tells us that 3 must be on the top face. When starting this kind of test, you may find it useful to mark on the example dice what numbers are on the hidden faces as we have done below.

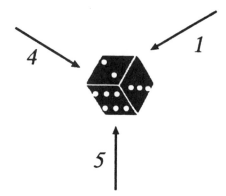

Rotation

This question type is similar to the principle of cubes and dice in that they are most easily solved by 'picturing' the rotation. Some children may find it useful to physically rotate the page.

	A	B	C	D	E

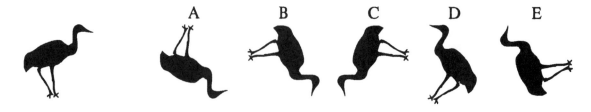

In this example using a silhouette of a stork, only the silhouettes under 'B' and 'E' can be rotated so that they are identical to the stork on the left. The other three storks are 'mirror' images of the same stork and are therefore wrong.

NON - VERBAL REASONING 1
ANSWER BOOKLET

ALPHA SERIES
PRACTICE PAPERS

GUIDANCE FOR PARENTS

The Alpha series is intended to provide children with the opportunity to become familiar with working on a range of examination papers. The style and content of the papers are appropriate for children in Years 6 and 7, i.e 10-12 years old. The papers are valuable aids for children who are due to sit examinations such as the 11+ and 12+.

Administering the Papers

It is important to select an appropriate time to give the test to your child. Choose an area which is well-lit, quiet and provide a table or desk for your child to work at.

The tests need to be timed. Please note that the examination time begins after the instructions have been read and understood.

Should you find that the recommended times are inappropriate for your child, they should be adjusted as appropriate. However the revised times should be adhered to for your child to gain experience of working under time pressure. It is useful if you can tell your child how much time is remaining at regular intervals and even more so for your child to learn to monitor the time for themselves. It is advised that you allow a gap of 2-3 days between each Paper.

Overall, the Practice Papers will be of most use where they are administered as closely to the actual examination conditions as possible.

Multiple-Choice Tests

This Alpha Series Pack contains multiple-choice type questions and the following should be observed.

Your child will need to enter his/her answers in the booklet and not on the test Papers themselves. A line should be drawn in the appropriate box thus ▭ using a pencil and any mistakes should be erased before the correct box is selected. This is important as in the actual test answers are scanned by a computer and a line left in an incorrect box will be marked as a wrong answer. There is obviously extra scope for errors as the child has to read the question sheet and the answer booklet simultaneously. He/she should be warned of this danger and encouraged to take particular care.

Finally, a raw score should be taken. Unfortunately, it is impossible to state what is a pass mark as a set number of children will be deemed to have passed the examination each year. Accordingly, the actual pass score will vary. Please note that some questions require two or more answers. Your child must get all parts correct in such cases as no half marks are awarded.

Similarities

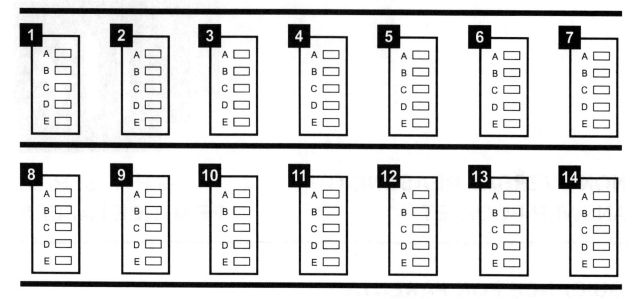

Cubes

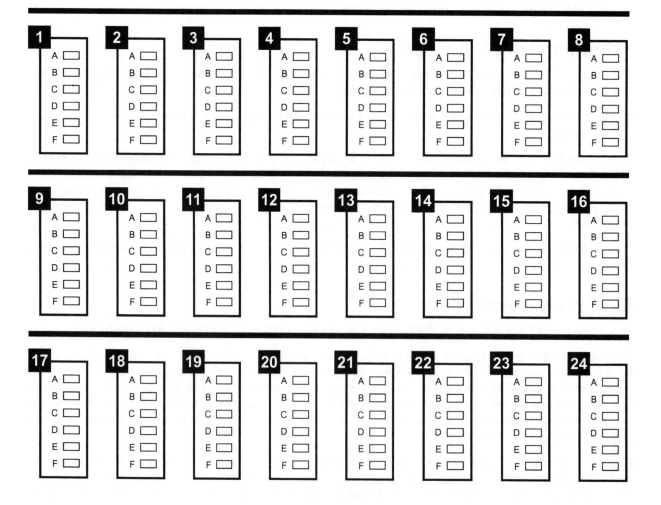

Shapes

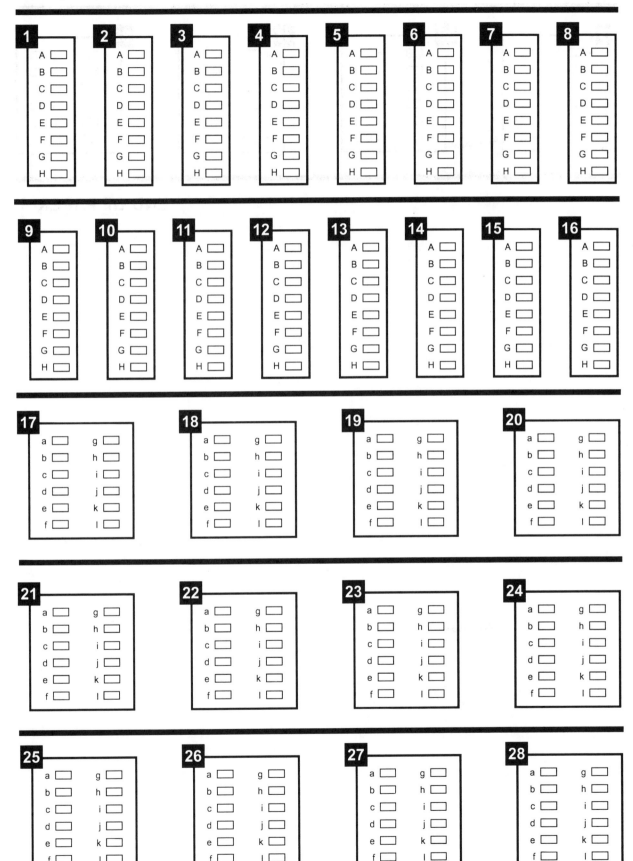

Shapes (Continued)

29

a ☐		g ☐	
b ☐		h ☐	
c ☐		i ☐	
d ☐		j ☐	
e ☐		k ☐	
f ☐		l ☐	

30

a ☐		g ☐	
b ☐		h ☐	
c ☐		i ☐	
d ☐		j ☐	
e ☐		k ☐	
f ☐		l ☐	

31

a ☐		g ☐	
b ☐		h ☐	
c ☐		i ☐	
d ☐		j ☐	
e ☐		k ☐	
f ☐		l ☐	

32

a ☐		g ☐	
b ☐		h ☐	
c ☐		i ☐	
d ☐		j ☐	
e ☐		k ☐	
f ☐		l ☐	

END OF PAPER 1

Analogies

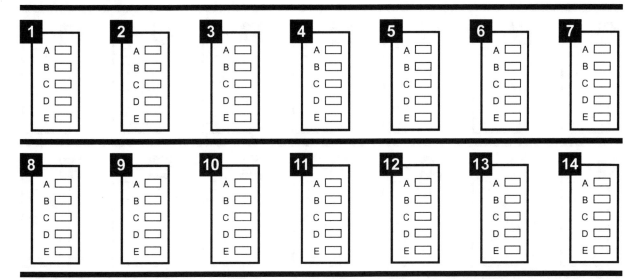

Flags

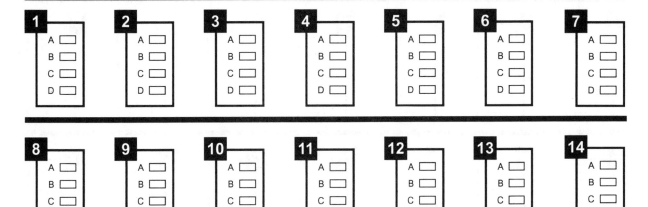

Similarities

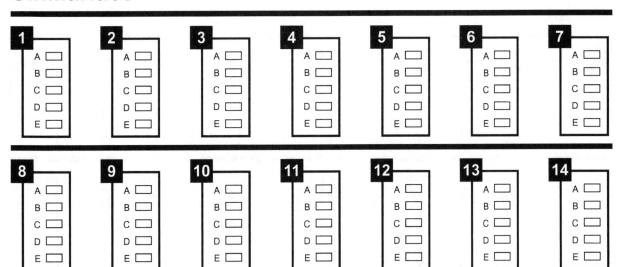

END OF PAPER 2

Odd-One-Out

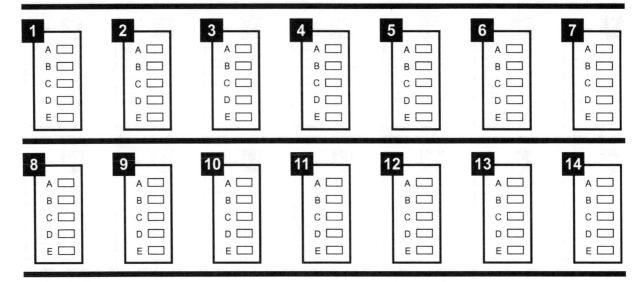

Rotation

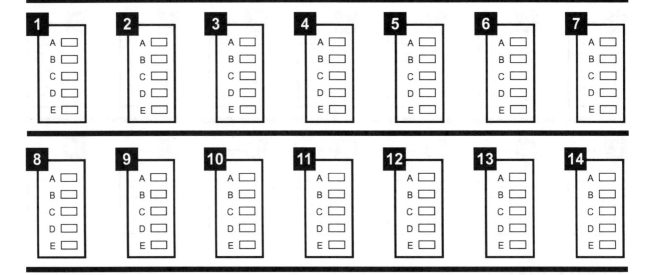

Series

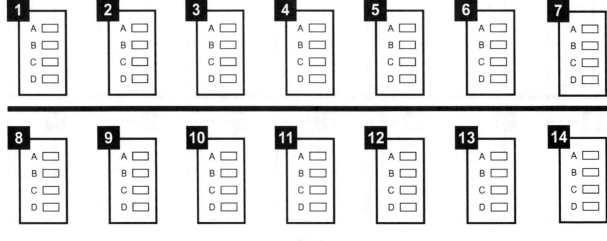

END OF PAPER 3

Silhouettes

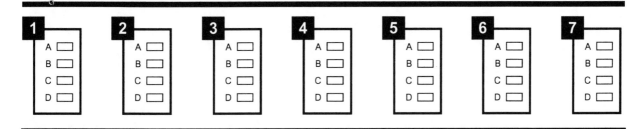

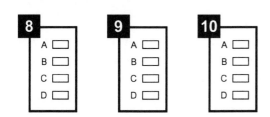

Analogies

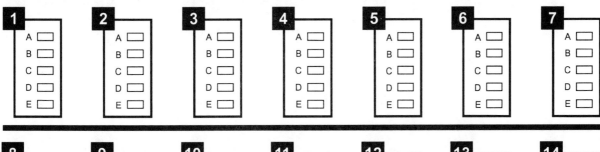

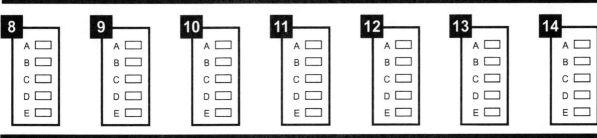

Series

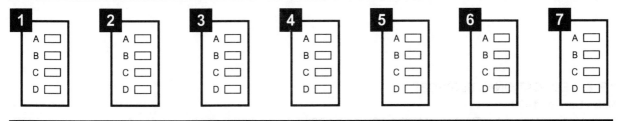

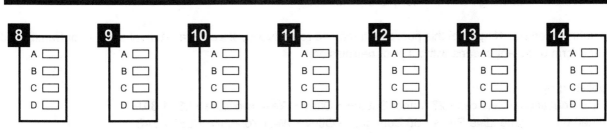

END OF PAPER 4

Published by:
R & S Educational Services • 23 Manor Square • Otley • West Yorkshire • LS21 3AP
Printed by - Chippendale Press • 65 Bondgate • Otley • West Yorkshire • LS21 3AB